247 Runtime

How to move your business to the cloud

to maximise profits

Sagar Rathod

Testimonials

"Sagar has decided to write this book as, in my experienced opinion, there appears to be a shortage of accessible advice for businesses surrounding technical knowledge. I believe my own extensive knowledge in the technological world would assist every business to earn more money and maximise their financial potential. This book is a great starting place for business owners wanting to find out more."

Jatin Rathod - Managing Director, CTA Graphics

"Sagar has set out clear points for you to utilise in assessing your business and to show you, how moving your business forward, can help your company to excel exponentially. This book is written in a non-technical way which makes it easier for the readers."

Michael Lewis - Library Service Manager

"I love that using the cloud can benefit all users from basic users to high demanding application usage. Sagar has helped me set my business to speed up data processing and marketing. I am able to concentrate on making sales instead of worrying about getting basic tasks done such as sending emails."

Hiten Bhatt – Director, BE GREAT

"This book has helped me personally with many tasks in all parts of my life. Using the cloud has helped me to be more organised and be more productive in communicating with other people and completing basic tasks. I have freed up more time and am able to spend more time with my family."

Martin White - Head Teacher, Waterfront Sports & Education Academy

"I am fascinated by the amount of energy it requires to setup a cloud infrastructure and maintain it with minimal technical knowledge. It is extremely easy and Sagar has shown clearly how to do this. This book will help any business who is looking to have easy manageability of applications and process."

Zee Survay – CEO, ZFit Leicester

About the Author

Sagar wrote this book to prove to himself what can be possible if you open yourself up to new opportunities.

He lives in the UK and is a freelancer as an IT & Audio-Visual Technician. Sagar has years of experience in the IT industry and is always eager to expand his knowledge and learn of new technology advances.

This book has been designed as a tool to start his entrepreneurial journey. Sagar has transformed from being a quiet individual, working behind the scenes, into a confident and bold person, with a desire to bring his professional identity into the business and corporate world, with the aim of wanting to support and guide others and share his knowledge and experiences.

He has participated in large events and has designed IT infrastructures for many different sized businesses. The people that have approached Sagar are always left satisfied.

Sagar believes that everyone should have basic technical knowledge, especially in our modern world. This is because technology is being used in every aspect of life. With the population growing exponentially it is essential that all people should know how to use a computer and a phone and be able to easily access the opportunities and facilities the World Wide Web can provide.

Foreword

You may have a different way of thinking, but I believe this book shows how a business can benefit financially. 247 Runtime contains specific examples on how to make a positive impact on the wider community.

This book will open your mind to new experiences and show you what products and technological developments could be used to make running your business more enjoyable and less stressful. With the understanding that taking the next step and changing your mind-set will get better results, can only result in more money at the end of the day.

This book will make you assess your business capabilities and turn it into a next generation nation.

Award Winning Entrepreneur,
CEO of Waterfront Sports & Education Academy
Michael Burgess

Dedication

This book is dedicated to all business owners that are reading this book.

The idea for writing this book came to me as there are huge amounts of businesses that are still running old school systems. We are now living in a modern age where we have vast amounts of technologies that are available to all. I believe that business owners do not have the requisite knowledge and are not aware of how important it is to use cloud computing. This will take your business to the next level.

I wrote this book to assist businesses in making the best decisions to maximize profits.

Acknowledgements

I would like to thank Hiten Bhatt for taking me on his entrepreneurial journey and inspiring me to start young as an entrepreneur. I would also like to thank Michael Burgess who has supported me by giving me the opportunity to excel in my skillset and for writing my foreword. I wouldn't have thought of trying to become the best version of myself that I can be, if it wasn't for my Guru Mahant Swami Maharaj, who has guided me through the toughest decisions in my life. My family have also been very supportive and have helped me in any way that they can so that I have a happy life.

Vishal Morjaria inspired me to write this book. He explained how writing a book can be used as a business card to promote yourself to the world. I thank Lyndsay Hill of The Brown Fox Bureau for her great editing skills and Haley James for designing the book cover.

Note to the Reader

The information, including opinion and analysis, contained herein is based on the author's personal experiences and is not intended to provide professional advice. The author and the publisher make no warranties, either expressed or implied, concerning the accuracy, applicability, effectiveness, reliability or suitability of the contents. If you wish to apply or follow the advice or recommendations mentioned herein, you take full responsibility for your actions. The author and publisher of this book shall in no event be held liable for any direct, indirect, incidental or consequential damages arising directly or indirectly from the use of any of the information contained in this book. All content is for information only and is not warranted for content accuracy or any other implied or explicit purpose.

Contents

~ Chapter 1 ~

How this Book will Benefit

your Business

In this book, I will explain what cloud computing is and how migrating to the cloud will benefit your business.

Some of you may not have heard of, or know, the meaning of cloud computing. Do not allow yourself to feel patronised by the word 'cloud'. In school, we learnt that a cloud is a white or grey object in the sky which contains condensed water vapour that floats around in the atmosphere. However, that is not what this book is about. Cloud computing is the way in which computer services are provided to the consumer. The word cloud suggests that the information floats in the air all around the world. Servers, storage, databases, networking, software, analytics and more are accessed through the internet.

There are many things that you can do using the cloud. In this book, I will explain some of the features of using the cloud to maximise profits for your business. I will explain that the cloud is split into three different services: SaaS

(Software as a Service); PaaS (Platform as a Service); and IaaS (Infrastructure as a Service).

SaaS – Software as a Service

SaaS is a term used in cloud computing. This is a method of delivering software over the internet. It is not stored locally in the company's premises, but rather stored in a datacentre, which are located all around the world. The application is available for the company to use on a subscription basis. Traditional software requires licences which are limited to a number of users or machines. The cloud providers install, maintain, upgrade and carry out all the security patching on the cloud machines. Users normally connect to the cloud by the web browser without the need to download any software, but some require plugins to run.

SaaS is a very big part of cloud services as it is the software that enables the application to meet the client's needs. Because of the cloud, applications do not need to be installed on every single machine on site. This also eliminates the process of having to reinstall software and configurations again when machines break down.

Some examples of SaaS include email and client/customer collaboration, customer relationship management, and healthcare relation applications. Other instances of SaaS consist of applications relating to accounting, invoicing and sales. SaaS allows all three applications to merge into one.

PaaS – Platform as a Service

PaaS is a framework in which third party companies can develop and customise applications which can then run in the cloud. This platform makes it easy to develop applications quickly, simply and cost-effectively. With this technology, cloud vendors can manage servers, operating systems, networking, and the PaaS software itself. Many businesses require PaaS for key services such as Java development and application hosting. PaaS can also be a virtualised system where engineers can use it to install Operating Systems and applications on. This feature also allows businesses to develop their own applications and enable them to have a separate offline system to update and use for testing, which does not affect the live version of the software.

The benefits of using PaaS is that businesses do not need to invest in hardware and do not need to employ IT experts to manage it. PaaS is able to adapt to the business's requirements and moves in agreement with cloud services. . It is flexible for users to use in a way that fits them best. By using the internet, developers can be located anywhere in the world but still be able to work on a specific project.

IaaS – Infrastructure as a Service

IaaS is the third service which makes up cloud computing. This is one of the most important, as it is the skeleton of the cloud infrastructure. Cloud vendors provide the hardware which is then managed by you. IaaS provides the servers, switches, routers, firewalls etc. They also handle operations such as updates, maintenance, backups and having redundancy in place. IaaS is suitable for temporary, experimental or changing scenarios. This service is based on a subscription which is calculated on an hourly, weekly or monthly basis.

IaaS is the physical building in which the cloud resides in. It is a massive datacentre, sometimes four times as big as a football field. IaaS contains the infrastructure for high demanding and high-performance applications to run on. Big Data is another term that is used in cloud computing, where computers calculate patterns and trends in the data. This service is a lot more cost effect then traditional server rooms. There are many advantages of using IaaS. As it can remove the need to have data centres and server rooms on site, keeping costs and space to a minimum, it is ideal for start-up businesses. IaaS also provides your business with better security using advanced encrypting algorithms. The service providers maintain the infrastructure which is reliable and meets SLAs (Service-Level Agreements).

This book will help you to understand these services and realise your ability to expand your business globally. The cloud will back up and store all your company's data which then can be accessed from anywhere in the world. It also has the option to set levels of permissions for users and different groups so that all information remains safe, confidential and secure. However, the key benefit is that all the data is available at your fingertips via your internet browser.

I will provide you with examples of how you can recruit members from all over the world by using the cloud infrastructure. This allows you to access a wider market of people and resources. The benefits of migrating will assist your business in becoming more connected by using collaborated applications. This allows you to access up-to-date reports on the progression of your company.

247Runtime will show you that the processing power does not need to be expensive and that you only need to pay for what you use. The cloud boosts productivity, as with all high intensive operations, which are handled by high speed servers in the cloud. The cloud is able to give much faster and accurate real-time data. The cloud gives flexibility to the end users who are tired of sitting in one place in front of the computer all day long. You will never need to worry about maintenance or upgrades as all this is carried out while your current applications and systems are online. This means that you are able to make money 24-7, 365 days a year. Businesses want to keep their doors open longer but are not physically able to do that. This is where cloud computing steps in. For a business, the current human expense to complete a basic task is costly, so why waste the money when a computer can do it for you. This means that your business is available to your clients all the time even when you are asleep. At the end of the day you are getting income regardless of your physical appearance in the office / headquarters.

<u>Reflective Questions</u>

1. What is Cloud Computing?

   ....

   ....

   ....

2. What is SaaS?

   ....

   ....

3. What is PaaS?

   ....

   ....

4. What is IaaS?

   ....

   ....

5. How do all of these services play a role in Cloud Computing?

   ....

   ....

   ....

<u>Notes</u>

....

....

....

....

....

....

....

....

....

....

....

....

....

....

....

....

....

....

~ Chapter 2 ~

Current Business Problems

Many businesses are not very productive in the way that they operate. Here I will detail possible issues which current business owners are facing. The number one reason is spending too much money on technology because the business owners have some, or very little, technical knowledge. They are trusting of their technical support teams, of whom which many have no, or very little, experience in this field and are not aware of current technology and the new software and systems available that can save money with the day-to-day running of the organisation.

Businesses spend a large amount of money on computer systems which can be replaced by using the internet for cloud services. Companies recruit IT support technicians to solve technical problems which results in a huge amount of money being paid out in salaries for these staff members. Money is regularly spent to fix problems because of a technical or hardware fault. This can be very expensive and the equipment can also be discontinued, resulting in the whole system needing to be changed.

Businesses also spend a lot of money on services that could be run within the cloud at a much lower cost, which I go into further detail in chapters four and six. This means that money is available to be spent elsewhere, such as taking your business to the virtual environment which would benefit everyone in the company.

How often have you been in the process of purchasing a product and then you come across the famous 404 error page, or the browser pops up saying that the service is currently unavailable or very busy. This happens when the servers are overloaded or have a system fault, which then takes time to recover from. There will be a massive queue of users waiting for permission to proceed. Often companies provide customer service telephone lines to communicate with customers but if this is affected by the downfall of internal systems, there is the risk of upsetting a lot of people, wanting to spend money. This is called 'Downtime'.

Downtime is where the business is running far slower than normal, or is at a halt because of a technical fault or human error, that can occur while configuring the systems. Another downtime could be when a company relies on a single person or team for technical support and they are unavailable. This can affect the running of the business if the IT technician is off sick and no other staff members in the company know how the system works. There could be harsh consequences for other areas of the company such as losing sales, resulting in reduced profits and wasted salary time with employees being left unoccupied.

This is the main problem for a business when, in the event of a disaster, systems are down and sales cannot be processed and staff are inactive. This results in further delays with delivering the product or service to the end user; preventing them from utilising the product or service resulting in reduced business, and essentially affecting the whole of the downward chain, upsetting hundreds if not thousands of people. The consequences could be costly resulting in compensation, wasted costs and downtime fees.

The way to reduce and eliminate any form of downtime, is to integrate your business to the cloud and use the computer services provided online via the internet. A key reason to make the move is because of the specialised people that are utilised to setup and maintain the servers in the cloud. This reduces the stress for the business as they have backup and redundant systems in place, so that there is 100% runtime.

The main objective of a business is to either solve a problem for the customer or provide a worthwhile product, but crucially it is to make a return which comes in the form of money. Another objective is for all clients to be happy so that they recommend the organisation to others, resulting in more sales and increased profit. The larger the income, the more that is available to invest in the company, by improving products or services, expanding their product base and rewarding staff by way of bonus and improved remuneration.

Another problem that businesses face is the threat of a cyber-attack. This can happen to any type of business and the main risk is when the IT technician does not know about network security and blocking miscellaneous activity from outside the network, as well as within the premises. This becomes a huge problem when employees are required to use laptops and tablets outside the workplace, such as when visiting clients or working from home. This then creates a legal problem as the company must obey the regulations of the Data Protection Act 1998, which is designed to protect employees' and customers' personal details. In the event of a cyber-attack, personal data can be stolen and sold for money or used fraudulently to destroy a person's online accounts and create false identities.

In this type of situation, the customers and potential clients lose trust in the business as it does not abide by the law and its ethos. This is a very serious matter which could lead to the closure of the company. Another issue that comes from less secure networks is that of hackers which use malicious scripts which can be run to shut down systems, delete important files, steal user account credentials and encrypt all data which cannot be recovered. This book will make you aware of how cloud computing can help you become more secure.

A very serious problem that many people face in the corporate world is having disputes between work colleagues. This could be due to communication breakdown, lack of social integration, and problems relating to religious beliefs and orientation, a common issue in today's society. A huge issue in this modern age is that the interaction between people has decreased due to digital media such as phones, tablets and computers. Managers are not using the right methods of communication to relay messages in the organisation hierarchy. This is because there is no system in place to monitor communications and make it better and more efficient. The employees are not able to access information easily and quickly. This results in slow decision-making processes and the meanings of information can become lost in translation.

Employees are not trained appropriately to use updated software and are left behind other competitors. Due to the lack of understanding of digital equipment and computer applications, particularly amongst more senior staff members, there can be inconsistences in delivering the service or product, which leads to a bad impression for the company.

Using the cloud can help eliminate these problems and can truly make your business stand out from the crowd. Read on to find out how!

As well as cyber-attacks, another threat in today's world is that of cyber threats. You may have heard that small and large corporations are regularly having their systems hacked. Many small and medium sized companies do not have the right amount of security in place. Many networks are left vulnerable to the outside world. Let me give you a few examples of some bad IT practices that happen in the workplace:

- The firewall allows unauthorised incoming traffic into the workplace network due to open ports on the network;
- There is no set standard for using strong passwords and logging out when not using the computer systems;
- The permissions are not set correctly for different user groups;
- Information and data is not encrypted;

Once an attacker has accessed your business network, it is very hard to stop them from destroying your data. This breaches the Data Protection Act and Data Misuse Act. This can particularly happen if businesses have outdated operating systems and non-supported equipment; or where laptops or mobile devices are stolen containing vital company information. Your company probably doesn't have content filtering for malicious websites.

The cloud is the easiest way to protect your company's information and is more respected now across the market. Read on to find out how this will help your business.

Reflective Questions

1. What problems are you facing in your business?

   ....

   ....

   ....

2. Do these relate to your business?

   ....

   ....

   ....

3. Would you like to make a change?

   ....

   ....

   ....

4. Are you happy with your current financial situation?

   ....

   ....

   ....

<u>Notes</u>

....

....

....

....

....

....

....

....

....

....

....

....

....

....

....

....

....

....

~ Chapter 3 ~

Efficiency

Moving to the cloud is an amazing experience. It feels like you are working in heaven. Your mind will be blown away when you find out what is possible in the technological world. You may first think that this is impossible, but before you make any kind of decision this book will explain step by step how this can be achieved.

The main benefit of moving your business to the cloud is that all of your information and applications are available 24-7 – 365 days a year. Your services are available all the time, even in an event of backups, maintenance and faults in hardware. By using the cloud, you are able to be more efficient. This plays a huge role in running the business, which ensures that all the systems are robust and working correctly so that you can provide the best service for your customers. Having all applications on the cloud, makes it easier for all employees to access information at any time, not only when they are physically in the office. This comes in very useful if visiting a client's location when their system does not allow external connections. The employees must then download all the data to the laptop, again a waste of their time. During this time, the pieces of data could be wrong or out of date. By using the cloud infrastructure, you are 100% guaranteed that all information is updated in real time.

Being able to know what is going on in the business is the owner's highest priority. By having business operations in the cloud makes it easier for business owners to know exactly what is going on and enable them to efficiently manage tasks and activities. Cloud computing also makes the life of the IT technician less stressful, as all configurations are in one place and can be accessed anywhere and at any time. All computer resources (e.g. networks, servers, storage, applications and services) that are on the cloud, can be rapidly configured and provided with minimal management effort and can be completed in less time.

There are current cloud systems that are easily manageable for all types of application and services. For virtual networking, a provider called Meraki have teamed up with

Cisco, a world leading hardware provider for routers, switches, firewalls, and wireless access points. Meraki have integrated the cloud infrastructure and made it easier for IT technicians, as well as normal employees who have no, or little, experience in using complex computer systems. Meraki have implemented their systems in many business types including the public sectors, education, small and medium businesses and large enterprise corporations.

Can you relate to a time where you have made a change to a document and then realised that you wanted the original document? This is where the cloud comes in. All businesses want is to have access to the changes that they have made in any type of document. The cloud system allows you to set up previous versions of the documents and configurations. This comes in handy when there is confusion between work colleagues, as well as customers. This is a type of proof and a way to clear up any confusion. The system is also another way to revert back if the configurations were incorrect and the service has stopped.

The main advantage of cloud computing is that all services are running all the time.

This feature in cloud computing allows the company to run very smoothly and is a life saver when operations are critically impaired. This feature runs simultaneously to day to day activities and does not affect the running of the business as all process are managed in the background. Managers of departments are also able to restrict certain users from reverting to a previous checkpoint.

In terms of customer service, this feature in the system can be beneficial for clients who access the company's systems and are able to see what changes have been made to the job, in real time, and by whom. This reassures the customer and proves that you are providing the best service for them; it is an interactive professional way for the client to view the status of the job, instead of sending emails back and forth.

Another problem that many businesses face are when the systems are down due to backups and maintenance. Using the cloud makes it feel like that this doesn't even happen. But in the real world this happens all the time as everything can be unpredictable. By using the cloud system to run your business, all the background operations can happen while the system is still in use. This is set up by using a duplicate system which is offline day-to-day and the upgrade is applied and tested by experienced engineers, only once it is fully working, is it then placed online for the company to use.

Backups are essential in the modern world of technology where issues and problems can occur unexpectedly. Data can be lost in many ways, such as a physical computer failure or a disaster such as a fire or flood in the building. It is not really economical or advantageous to recover data once it has been changed or deleted. The company can decide when backups are undertaken. This entirely depends on how important the data is. Using cloud computing makes backup tasks very easy, only a few clicks are required to setup a backup and restore the system.

You would not want to be in a situation where employees are waiting for the systems to be back online in order to get on with their duties. As a result of this downtime customers can be lost and money is wasted in buying new equipment.

How many times have you faced a situation where your current system fails or is not working properly due to a hardware fault. This becomes a serious problem as businesses would not be able to run efficiently. There are many reasons why physical systems fail, such as a power supply failure, a corrupt hard drive, overheated processors or corruption in the operating system registry, to name but a few. By migrating to the cloud, you will be eliminating this problem as the company who hosts your cloud environment, will be the ones that deal with these issues. The infrastructure is setup in such a way that there are redundant components all the time, an important facility to have available in case some of the components fail and effect the running of the service.

This also helps to keep the business running all of the time, crucial when the company has employees and customers all around the world. The cloud is more reliable in terms of performance and availability. Once migrated to the cloud, there will be less computer hardware in the premises to manage and the hardware you do have will be simple to use. You are able to have copies of your data in multiple sites which can be recovered or moved in the event of a disaster. This will also save money by spending less on computer equipment.

Nowadays, computer engineers spend most of their time racking and stacking servers and switches. They are not using their time and energy efficiently. Cloud computing removes the need for many of those tasks which allows the team to achieve business goals. The cloud allows the company to adapt to different situations. If user demand increases, cloud services can rise to meet the demands, and can then just as easily be decreased as demand drops. Thus, eliminating the problem of over-provisioning or IT systems overload.

The cloud allows users to design and organise their own desktops. This increases productivity as they are more comfortable using their own computers and laptops. Users are able to work in a way that fits them best. With the cloud, you are able to do what you do best. Cloud computing offers the company to expand and accept large amounts of data which is made easy to use. The systems are capable of this type of application.

<u>Reflective Questions</u>

1. How will becoming efficient help your business?

   ....

   ....

   ....

2. What are the ways in which it will benefit your company?

   ....

   ....

   ....

3. What will you change to make this happen?

   ....

   ....

   ....

<u>Notes</u>

....

....

....

....

....

....

....

....

....

....

....

....

....

....

....

....

....

....

~ Chapter 4 ~

Money Saver

Businesses want to save money in all departments of the company. This can be seen all over the world, especially where the governments are cutting budgets in education and medical care. The main object for any business is to make a profit and expand to a larger market. Migrating to the cloud can benefit the business by cutting costs. Some ways of saving money are explained below, but a key expense for most businesses, is the huge amount of money spent on running servers and computer systems, which can be eliminated if moved to the cloud.

Servers use high levels of power and energy which is always reflected in the electricity bill. Many companies cannot manage with only one server but have multiple, on occasions enough to fill up a small classroom. Cloud computing allows businesses to have minimal hardware onsite. This saves on energy bills and costs which can be used to run the business more efficiently to meet client needs. As technology advances, hardware becomes outdated and needs to be upgraded. Enterprise equipment is not cheap. By using the cloud infrastructure, it reduces these issues because the vendors are the ones that do this for you.

You may have dozens of servers for individual services that the company needs. In the cloud, most servers are virtualised so less servers are used, which means less energy is used. This is a better way of utilising processing power and storage space. Servers are much more powerful than normal desktop machines and are able to run more than one server at a time without a decrease in performance.

Servers require certain conditions to work well. They create lots of heat and the processor needs to be kept cool for it to do the work. Companies invest lots of money on air conditioning to keep the server room cool. Many companies use old server equipment that uses lots of power. Upgrading to new equipment means that it is more energy efficient, effectively using less energy. Using the cloud reduces the amount of electricity used in the office, as most of the applications are running in the cloud, so there is no need for high powered servers.

In mission critical scenarios, businesses require 24-7 IT support and they may have to spend more money to have more staff in place. By utilising cloud services, your business will be able to save money because not as many IT support engineers will be required. Salaries are one of the highest annual expenditures for businesses and having less staff reduces labour costs. By eliminating routine maintenance, the IT team can focus more of their time on improving business work flow. In the case of small sized companies, by moving to the cloud you are able to reduce the IT team to a minimum and reduce the need to hire third party people to fix the hardware.

By having less hardware on the company's premises means that you will be using less office space. This results in lower rent and energy bills. For small business and those that are starting up, funds are tight and they cannot afford to spend money on large office spaces or a fully configured

IT infrastructure. This is where the cloud services can be implemented to save costs. This amount of capital can be invested into the business instead to create a better product or service.

Many companies do not remain in the office all of the time, they are most likely out on the road meeting clients or visiting suppliers. The office would be left empty and not utilized properly. Servers use lots of power, energy and create noise pollution, which is not ideal for employees to work in. The cloud makes the life of the employee much easier as they do not need to worry about the machines and applications not working.

The benefit of using the cloud is that you only need to pay for what you use. This analogy is like a PAYG (pay-as-you-go) SIM card. Many cloud service providers use a monthly or yearly payment system. They calculate the rate depending upon the business's needs. Some providers may specifically base this on how many servers you require or how much RAM (Random Access Memory) your applications require and how much storage space you need. The advantage of this is that there are no wasted resources. With traditional enterprise setups, the machines are always running at full power. However, by using the cloud, it allows you to change how much storage or processing power that you need at the current time, ideal when a business is growing year-on-year and requirements increase.

Many cloud providers price their service depending upon the amount of hardware required, or the number of users that will be using it, known as licences. This mean that the vendors are automatically assigning the hardware dependent upon the client's requirements. Most of the decisions are made externally so that you, as a business owner, do not need to worry about the technical aspects of the service that you need in order to run in the cloud.

I have talked about many ways of saving money. Now what do you do with the money that you have saved? This can be invested back into the business – a great way to keep on top of your game. Your business will be able to excel and expand in all areas. Investing back into your business allows you the opportunity to learn and experience new ways of processing your products or services. In the end, the business profits will increase which will then lead to higher salaries and happier staff. The employees will be more productive creating a seamlessly happy working environment.

Technology companies realise that business owners want the simplest way to provide the best products and services to their clients. The cloud is the new generation of information management and service providing.

<u>Reflective Questions</u>

1. Are you currently spending more money than you are making?

    ....

    ....

    ....

2. What would you change in your business?

    ....

    ....

3. How would you implement this in your business?

    ....

    ....

    ....

4. How much could you save?

    ....

    ....

    ....

<u>Notes</u>

....

....

....

....

....

....

....

....

....

....

....

....

....

....

....

....

....

~ Chapter 5 ~

Spend Time Wisely

"Time Is Money"

Many successful business people abide by this quote. If time is spent doing the wrong things, then this will cost the business lots of money. Time is precious and you cannot get it back. This is another reason why cloud computing will be extremely helpful for the business. In this context, the quote means that if you are spending time fixing computers then you are not making sales, which results in lack of profit. This is not good for any business as the main goal is to make a profit and expand. Employees need to make the most of the time in the office by working and producing results, instead of waiting around for the system to work.

Managers of departments in large organisations should not need to spend large amounts of time emailing IT support, trying to explain the situation that the computer is not working or that they are not able to send or receive emails. The manager's role is to make sure the staff are working together as a team and not complaining about technical problems. This is where cloud computing comes in place.

The cloud platform is robust and easy for everyone to use. It is integrated to support many internet browsers. Many cloud applications are written in Java or C++ (common everyday coding applications), which are highly compatible with many operating systems across all markets.

How do you make money in any company? Sales obviously! If you are spending more time fixing problems relating to a technical error, then your main focus is not on the customer. To achieve higher profits, you must be spending the majority of your time closing down sales and selling your products. The cloud makes it very simple for you and your business. All information and applications are stored on extremely reliable server infrastructures. This reduces the need to set up new servers and computers. Most of the employees would prefer to use their own laptops or tablets. This saves time because the engineers do not have the need to fix office-based machines when they stop working. The IT team do not need to maintain machines as this is done by the individual using their own devices.

The company has the freedom to spend more time with clients and in a way which fits them best. The cloud really helps as everything can be accessed through the internet so that employees are able to provide much better customer service. A good system plays a huge part in the customer's eyes. If they feel that they are taken care of and you are able to solve their problems, they will come back. This results in more sales. This could also lead to them recommending you on a social marketing level, a great free advert for your business – social media and social marketing are just as important today as the cloud itself.

Work Smarter Not Harder

Have you ever been in a situation where your pieces of data are not in the right format for the updated systems? Or a time where you get an email from the IT department that at a certain time you will face a system downtime due to weekly maintenance and upgrades? Having to hire extra staff to carry out these manual tasks. The cloud eliminates this problem for your business. Currently this is done abroad on the Eastern side of the world where labour is cheap. However, this does not eliminate the time factor. Again, time is money. If you are not spending time more efficiently then there will be less cash inflow and more cash outflow. No business wants to be inefficient, this is why I am writing this book. This has made you aware that there is another option which has been heavily tested and is used by many companies across the world. However, many companies have still not implemented the cloud into their systems yet.

The sooner you migrate to the cloud the more cost effective it would be for your business and will save you time in the future. The cloud allows you to share information in just a few clicks. It also has the ability to work as part of a team to complete a project much faster. This is explained in more detail later in the book.

If you could work from your phone or tablet instead of a desktop computer, how much time could you save yourself? This means that you are able to work while you are travelling, such as on trains and planes, or whilst out and about such as cafes and coffee shops whilst meeting clients – in fact in any out of office location.

Have you ever lost your dairy or pocket calendar or your phone is stolen, broken or lost? What happens then...

There are many cloud applications that you can implement in your business. A couple of widely used ones include Google Calendar, Office 365 and iCloud. These applications will help you keep organised and assist with time management. This is extremely important particularly when managers and employees are required to attend meetings, in various locations. Many client meetings take place out of the office, especially when trying to secure new business. Using the cloud helps schedule meetings, events and tasks that need to be completed on a certain day. Google Calendar is used worldwide because of the simplicity of the user interface. It is compatible with Android, IOS and Computers. You are able to set permissions so that certain people have access, allowing a person to see and edit the contents of a calendar, which is perfect for a secretary or administrative assistant who takes care of the scheduling. And Google Calendar has the option to send out emails to remind individuals about meetings or events.

Something to remember is that time doesn't stop. If you are not in the office it doesn't mean that your business stops making money. The cloud gives you the freedom to spend time doing things that you need to do, instead of being physically at the office managing the business. Knowing that when you go sleep your business is still operating without you and making profits is an amazing feeling. Using the cloud, you can still make bank transfers using online services such as PayPal.

Reflective Questions

1. Are you spending time efficiently?

   ....

   ....

2. How much time could you save by using the cloud?

   ....

   ....

3. What would you change?

   ....

   ....

   ....

4. What platform would be beneficial for your business?

   ....

   ....

   ....

<u>Notes</u>

....
....
....
....
....
....
....
....
....
....
....
....
....
....
....
....
....
....

~ Chapter 6 ~

Uses of Cloud Computing

In this chapter, you will get a sense of the current products and services that already exist in the cloud and which can be implemented straight away without too much configuration. Some of these applications are free, which really is a plus point for new businesses who do not have much capital to spend on cloud applications. The nice thing about cloud computing is that you only pay for what you require and what you use. This means that you are not contracting to software licences and hardware that you do not need.

The example shown below will illustrate how to implement these applications into your business to save money, time and energy. You will become more productive. There are also platforms that you can customise and edit to meet your company's needs. In this book, I will give examples of the main business needs and what is available to us right now.

The main reason for having a computer setup in any business is because they need a place to store their data and swiftly communicate with the outside world. More companies use storage servers and NAS devices (network attached storage) to keep their data. The problem with this method of storage is that it requires space and regular maintenance. By using the cloud, you do not need to worry about it taking up a full room in your building or a large amount of space on your desk. Other problems would not occur if storage was dealt with on the cloud, such as failed hard drives and storage expansion. The IT department do not need to spend time managing the hard disks and replacing them once they show bad sectors. All of this is done by the cloud vendors.

Some of the providers for cloud storage are Google Drive, One Drive, iCloud Storage, Dropbox, Box and WeTransfer. Each one of these services has its advantages and disadvantages. In this book, I am going to talk about Google Drive and OneDrive as these platforms are most used in the business world.

Google Drive gives regular users 15GB of storage, free of charge. It also supports many file formats such as Microsoft Word and Excel documents, PowerPoint, Adobe Acrobat, MP3 and video files (MP4). This is very useful for businesses as most of the regularly used file types are compatible to view online without the need to install software or plugins. Nowadays, these file types are available on most smartphones. This allows the user to easily access their preferred media to do that job. Another reason to use Google Drive is the ability to share your files with people that you trust, such as work colleagues and clients. It gives you the option to set certain permissions for different people. If you are questioning the security of the files, then do not worry. Google believes that obtaining trust from their customers they must protect their privacy. This is why all documents are encrypted using 'SSL' which is a security protocol that establishes an encrypted link between the server and the browser. Finally, Google has thought about situations when users are in places with little or no internet connection availability so you can also use your files offline. To get more storage, Google have setup a monthly payment system where you pay for the storage that you need.

Another online application for online storage is WeTransfer. This is a very good tool to use to allow people to send small sized files, up to 2GB of data, very quickly. The free version of this service has a cap of 2GB, whereas the enterprise plan has a limit of sending a file or multiple files up to 20GB. The package offers more functionality such as password protection, customized options and long-term storage instead of the seven day option in the free version. This tool is used widely by graphic designers, for example, who send their edits to their clients to see the progress of work. There is no signing up or login required to view the files. All the files are sent via email with a link for the end user to download. This means that an email is sent for both the customer and yourself, so that you have a backup of the files. All files are shared securely.

Another highly used service is web hosting. This can be a standalone website or a series of applications. Web hosting is a large topic but in this book, I am going to tell you the basic information to allow you to make the decision of what is required to bring your company to the next stage and increase your presence online. By hosting your website on the cloud, this provides you with the flexibility to change and update your information easily. Another reason is that the web hosting service providers use top level encryptions to secure your website, this could be a simple website just providing information to the customer or a custom designed dynamic website where pages are created in real-time and the information is stored in a database. The cloud allows you to create dynamic websites, advantageous for larger businesses who may require hundreds or thousands of pages with complex text and imagery. Many webmasters nowadays provide a range of services besides hosting websites. Some of the services are domain names, emails, and storage. Some examples are, GoDaddy, 123-Reg and 1-On-1. For more information of how to setup a website please visit this area on my website:

www.247runtimebook.com

Blogs are another type of media by which businesses talk to their clients. WordPress is an opensource tool where you can create blogs and websites using inbuilt themes or third-party themes. There are thousands of plugins that are available which can help you customise your site such as SEO (Search Engine Optimization), multi-functional tables and multimedia. Google loves WordPress sites, because they are updated regularly and the content is in a logical format. WordPress has a huge community of developers and designers who are willing to help you create the best website for your business. Many webmasters support WordPress as it is widely used.

Many businesses who have websites are missing one thing, an eCommerce site to sell their products and services. The reason to use the cloud to host this is because you want your clients to trust your site and purchase from you. PayPal is one of the most secure ways of buying products or services and transferring funds to another person online. ECommerce is a faster way to purchase products from your business. This feature allows your business to grow globally as your products and services are available on the internet worldwide. You will be saving money on labour as most of the processes are carried out automatically by the cloud. Many businesses do not have a physical location in which they operate as all the tools are available online. This means that the business is easy to start and manage. Some opensource e-Commerce platforms that you can use are Magento, Spree and OpenCart.

All businesses require an email facility. Emails are used to communicate to people within the company as well as to the outside world such as customers, suppliers and reaching out for new business. Emails have been used for some time now and are used every single minute of every day across the world. Emailing provides speedy communication so that people can make quick decisions and the processing of products and services is much faster. Emails are a cheap way of communicating as every business has broadband and all that emails require, is the internet. Another reason emails are used in business is to keep track of what decisions are being made, to send out minutes to members who attended a meeting and for those that were not able to. Emails can be used as proofs when a mistake is made or there is some confusion.

There are many email providers on the market such as Gmail, Yahoo Mail, Outlook, Mail.com and iCloud mail. All of the above are very similar but they also have their differences. However, for business users you would not want to use their free version for emails. How would you like your business email to be 247runtimebook@gmail.com? This does not look very professional. Instead you would want to use info@247runtimebook.com. All businesses should purchase a domain for their company. The domain is a type of identity to the whole world. This is how your business can be found on the internet where millions of websites reside. A domain name adds credibility to your business. People trust your sites and emails which have a personalised domain name, not a generic one that is provided by your email provider.

There are many places to look when you want an email account with your own domain. I am going to explain some of the existing email companies that provide business class emails. The first one is G-Suite which is part of Google. G-Suite provides many applications which I will cover in more detail in the coming chapters. One section of G-Suite is Gmail for Businesses. This package includes 30 GB of inbox storage, customer email support and is also compatible with Microsoft Outlook and other email providers. It does not have adverts, which is a great relief, as you want to concentrate on your work, not be distracted by adverts. G-Suite also allows you to conduct meetings with up to fifteen people just from your email account. Gmail is compatible on most devices such as Android, IOS and most web browsers. Again G-Suite has a subscription-based payment, either monthly or yearly.

Another service provider is Microsoft with Office 365. This is another cloud platform where many applications can be used from the internet. Outlook is the email service that they provide. Office 365 is another provider of customized emails for business use. There are some differences between the G-Suite and Office 365. However, it is the other applications on the platform that determine what the business chooses to fulfil their needs. OneDrive for business is a great tool for sharing and storing data. It incorporates well with Outlook and other applications in Office 365.

Another type of cloud application that many businesses use is the ability to stream music and videos. The most common streaming medias include YouTube, Vimeo and Sound Cloud. Businesses use YouTube, for example, to upload videos to promote their products and services. With G-Suite this makes your life very easy as everything is synced and in one place. YouTube is the most popular site that is used to stream videos. This creates a whole new target market to sell your products. YouTube is also used in the corporate world where you can upload pitching videos of new products and the video is available anywhere where there is internet. For example, schools and universities use YouTube videos for tutorials to help students understand the topic better. It is a visual aid to explain a complex concept.

The internet is getting faster and faster. In many developed countries, you can get speeds of up to 100Mbps to 1Gbps for business lines. This means that you can upload and download multiple photos and videos at the same time.

A key sector that uses the cloud are the Education Departments across the world. There are two main cloud applications that they use to teach by way of online tutorials, taking exams and learning through interaction, which are BlackBoard and Moodle. Schools, colleges and universities use technology to engage with the students. Youths nowadays use computers and smartphones more than ever. Year by year, more and more teenagers are using technology and social media to interact with each other. Using cloud applications such as BlackBoard and Moodle, help students with certain topics, test their knowledge and also aid disabled students.

BlackBoard is a Virtual Learning Environment. It is used by both teachers and students. Teachers use it to setup their curriculum and add media such as photos, videos, audio clips and worksheets. BlackBoard has features such as a discussion board so that it is easy for students to get hold of teachers and other students if they are struggling or need to ask a question. Using BlackBoard saves money for schools as all the learning books and materials are online and can be viewed at school and at home.

Businesses can also use these applications for training and development purposes. You are able to set courses online for employees to undertake in their spare time allowing them to be up to date with training and certifications. This saves time and money on the need to hire people to conduct training sessions, requiring office space and taking up valuable work time. You can see the individual's progress and what their weaknesses are so they can improve on them.

Reflective Questions

1. What are the uses of cloud computing?

   ....

   ....

   ....

2. Which application/service would you use?

   ....

   ....

   ....

3. How will this application/service help your business?

   ....

   ....

   ....

4. What are your feeling right now?

   ....

   ....

   ....

<u>Notes</u>

....

....

....

....

....

....

....

....

....

....

....

....

....

....

....

....

....

....

~ Chapter 7 ~

Team Collaboration

In this chapter, I am going to explain how moving your applications to the cloud can help your work teams and groups collaborate better. This chapter will help your company to become more like a family, encouraging people to work together and support each other, instead of any feelings of unrest. By using these application in your business on a daily basis it will help your staff cooperate and work together.

Using applications such as G-Suite and Office 365 can help aid communication between colleagues. In our modern working world, with businesses operating 24-7, not all of the team is always available to attend the office at the same time when working on a project. It is also of assistance when day-to-day events occur such as sickness, injury and death, requiring individuals to perhaps work from home. The cloud packages assist the team by still keeping communication lines open and updating them, allowing work to be delegated to others easily and stress-free. As all the work is updated and kept in the cloud, all the information is available to team leaders as well as managers.

You will be able to use different types of medium to communicate with others. Other options that could help your delivery may be video conferencing between the team or individuals. Another example is group chat rooms where team members can use this service to talk to each other about their progress and also ask if they need help on a particular task. You can also conduct a conference call for all of your staff where ever they may be. This is a very quick and effortless process to relay important information. Using the cloud, you can be sure that all of your interactions between each other are encrypted and safe from anyone intercepting it.

There are many existing applications that can help you to manage the people that work for you. It is said that a great leader produces a great worker. By using the cloud, you are able to create daily tasks for individuals or those in a team project. An example of this application is Slack and

Trello. Being able to set aims and objectives from the touch of a finger is great and saves you time. This also provides proof and a record of instructions so there can be no confusion of what has been asked of those individuals. You are able to select certain users to view certain information and set levels of access for those who are working in a team. This tool comes in handy when you are working on a critical project where all the team members need to be aware of important information as all the data is stored in one place and can be ordered specifically, as to what is more important.

Many businesses find it very hard to keep track of what is happening in their company. By using a cloud system, you can integrate it with other applications. A prime example of what all business owners look for is to ascertain how much profit it is turning over. Cloud applications can be used to give you live updates and reports on how many sales are made every day and also what your costs are. By using the cloud to do all of the crucial and time-consuming tasks, this saves time and energy. This can also save money as you would not need to recruit people to carry out this type of work. This helps in eliminating human error and provides the ability to complete the task faster.

Many businesses have a Human Resource (HR) Department. This department is responsible for recruiting new members of staff, managing training and resources for existing staff, and dealing with the more delicate issue of dismissal and redundancy. The cloud can be used in these situations to measure the performance of each individual in the business. The cloud gives you the ability to obtain information from many different sources and put them in one place. You can also create your own database of all the individuals and design forms which then can be used to show data and trends in graphs and charts. The beauty of using the cloud is that you can use any computer to enter these details and also share your finding with your relevant people, such as managers and leaders. This can be used as a record for any decision that a company makes. There are many applications that measure performance of the business and produce end of year reports to show directors, managers and shareholders.

In team collaboration, team members must be able to access information from each other. The cloud makes this seamless. By using a shared storage space on the internet this can save so much time and money. Many people still transfer files from computer to a USB pen drive and give it to their colleges who are just sitting next to them. By using shared storage, you are able to send and receive files instantly. However, this highly depends on the file size and network speeds. In these situations, there are certain things that you need to consider. This includes how secure the transmission of the medium is. Important information such as customer details, bank details and classified documents can be stolen and used fraudulently against the company and its customers. This is breaking the Data Protection Act and can result in customers being unhappy with your service, meaning that they will leave your business, resulting in reduced sales and less profit. Using USBs for file transfer poses a risk of losing it and/or for it to become corrupted. This can cause process delays and wasted costs.

There are many existing applications in the cloud that you can use in your business. These applications are setup so that you can be up and ready in just a few minutes. The cloud allows you to setup multiple shared folders for many clients from just the click of a finger. You do not need to go to every single device to configure the settings. All information can be accessed through the web browser where there is internet availability.

The cloud can also help you create a bigger network. This will help you in all areas of the business, especially in securing quality contacts who then can help you make more money. You can express your feelings about a subject in the discussions page, which can be accessed through any device such as a phone or laptop. It is very important that you can communicate with people from your smartphone. This is where the cloud fits in! As you are able to text, call and send files to anyone from your mobile. When you are at a networking event and someone would like to know more about your business, you are able to show your website and products from your phone. It will reflect a professional identity for your business, showing you have invested money in technology to advance itself and reach more people. When working as a team on a project, the use of cloud applications can help individuals connect by finding out who is doing similar tasks and who you can learn from.

In certain situations, businesses lose money because of human error and unexpected circumstances. By using cloud applications, you can still run your business as usual. This will help your business to have no or minimal downtime. As many leaders claim, a business with no single point of failure is a great business. This means that you are confident that when things do not go the way you want to, you have set up a system to work around it - you are ready when a disaster strikes and there is an economical swift solution to enable your business to keep functioning, keeping your customers happy and making money. Using the cloud can help you with this. A system can be setup whereby a system records what task or job everyone does. This makes it easier for managers to look back and find information that could relate to an employee while they are off sick or not able to come into the office. The system allows employees to work from remote locations and continue as if they were still in an office environment.

You are able to assign the project to another member to take over. This is very easy to do as all of the information and files are in one place and can be viewed by the new user from their computer. The only thing that is required is to allow the person access to that piece of information. This can be done from the administrator dashboard. This is the backbone of the system. It is where you can define permissions and attributes for groups and users. This can all be done from a web browser on the internet.

Reflective Questions

1. Give an example where there was confusion?

   ....

   ....

   ....

2. How can technology help you reduce this?

   ....

   ....

   ....

3. How can you work as a team more productively?

   ....

   ....

   ....

4. What kind of system would you like to implement?

   ....

   ....

   ....

<u>Notes</u>

....
....
....
....
....
....
....
....
....
....
....
....
....
....
....
....
....
....

~ Chapter 8 ~

Virtual Environment

The cloud allows you to run your business from anywhere in the world. You could be taking a holiday in the Caribbean, sailing round the Mediterranean, or backpacking across South America and still be able to run your company. You are able to log into your own workspace from outside of the work premises and access all of your documents, emails and contacts. A feature in cloud computing is virtual machines. Using virtual machines can help businesses when managing lots of servers, computers and networking equipment. Virtual machines are a replacement of client computers. Many employees do not like to use work computers as they can be very slow, contain viruses and it can be frustrating using something different. The cloud allows each individual user to use which ever device that they prefer and they can then log into the virtual machine to use the company's applications and information. Virtual machines have many good factors, such as using less electricity, less equipment and little money is required to invest into IT equipment.

The advantage of using virtual machines are that they can be easily managed without moving to different locations where the local computers are. All this can be done through the network. Cloud computing uses technology to dynamically adapt to situations so that the business applications are always running without performance loss and memory allocation. For example, in a data centre where they use virtualization, the IT staff will create a new virtual machine or use a dormant one, based on the business's needs, such as starting a new project. Virtual machines are used as it provides application provisioning to automate the deployment of custom application configurations, high availability and disaster recovery options. Each virtual machine can run independently as well as in a cluster for larger projects and high performance and redundant solutions.

There are many applications that you can use for virtualization. Some of them are Windows Hyper-V, VMware Cloud, Cisco Virtual Application Cloud Segmentation and also Citrix Cloud. All these applications provide Infrastructure as a Service. VMware Cloud allows you to integrate the cloud with your current setup in your work environment.

Nowadays, more and more applications are becoming available in the cloud. You can now use most of the Microsoft Office applications in the cloud through Office 365. As mentioned before, you can share calendars, files, pictures and videos through social media. Google Analytics is often used by businesses that track websites and mobile website traffic. Other applications that are hosted in the cloud is Adobe Creative Cloud. This piece of clever engineering from Adobe allows professional designers to work in a team on the same project, at the same time, to share resources and create 'on the go'. Many adobe users have claimed that Creative Cloud is the best thing that Adobe ever did. It helps freelancers increase their productivity and workflow to increase their contracts and finish them off quicker with better quality.

Another application that many businesses use is Sage, which is a piece of software used for accounts, payroll and business management solutions. Sage has now become available for cloud users. There were many problems for using offline software as to access it you must install the software using a CD Drive. On the CD box it provides the system requirements meaning you must then use a computer that is compatible with this software. You then need to insert the activation code or licence to use the program. Another issue with using a local version of the software is that all the data is stored on the client machine. This brings various problems as there is often not a backup of the records if the computer were to be stolen or broken.

Content Management Systems is an application used to manage information digitally. CMS's are used mainly by large companies where they have thousands or tens of thousands of records and content material that they need to store in a logical way. The cloud is mainly used in this scenario. The advantage of using a Content Management System in your business is that you are able to index all your data where you can easily search for information and the system pulls out the content in which ever format that you require. This could be a word document, PDF or in an Excel spreadsheet. Using this system, you can easily add, change, delete and update records without the need to create the whole thing again. You are able to make customized templates, have group-based permissions for users to have access to certain pieces of data and high availability as it can be accessed over the internet. It also reduces the need to code these processes from scratch. CMS have the ability to create a unified look and feel that matches your company's identity and branding.

Some Content Management Systems that are available on the market are AgilityCMS, Drupal, Magnolia and dotCMS.

Email Marketing is something that you may or may not have heard of. Many businesses are not using this facility properly and is why they are not able to make more profit. Email marketing is a tool that businesses use to keep current and new clients up to date with their products and services. Using cloud applications to automate email messages and create responses can be greatly beneficial for your business.

MailChimp is one of the best and free applications for email marketing. In MailChimp you can create personalised templates that you can use over and over again with many customers at once. There are many options for you to insert text, pictures and videos. You can also add HTML codes for more complex looking emails. The best thing about MailChimp is that you can create different lists of email address that you would like to use regularly. These lists will eliminate the use of using excel spreadsheets using the import function. This allows you to create subscriber lists instantly using your current system. You are also able to export the setting for backups and for use in other cloud applications. You may have a weekly or monthly newsletter. This amazing application allows you to schedule all emails so that they can be sent without you even being there to physically send it.

Other platforms that are great for email marketing and analysing email traffic are Hubspot, InfusionSoft and Marketo. For more information about these platforms please go to my website www.247runtimebook.com.

The cloud allows you to have virtual assistants who are available 24-7 to help employees, as well as customers. A Virtual assistant is an individual that is able to assist clients from a remote location. This is really beneficial as all businesses want to expand their business and make it available globally. Due to different time zones, your business can have multiple virtual assistants in different countries as customer support. This gives you an advantage over your competitors as you are available to your customers all of the time. Great customer service equates in the happy customer, which results in more profits.

You can sell your products in different countries and be sure that they are taken care of by having the customer support from someone able to speak their language. This makes it personal and your business is providing a bespoke, individual service, giving excellent value for money, with the result that they will hopefully come back for more. The money will follow if the fundamentals are set properly. The cloud can help you create a great infrastructure for your business to grow and expand and maximise profits.

Reflective Questions

1. How will virtual machines and applications elevate your business?

   ....

   ....

   ....

2. How will this help you and your business?

   ....

   ....

   ....

3. In what ways will this maximise your profits?

   ....

   ....

   ....

4. Where do you see your company in the next five years?

   ....

   ....

   ....

Notes

....
....
....
....
....
....
....
....
....
....
....
....
....
....
....
....
....

TO FIND OUT HOW THE CLOUD CAN HELP YOUR BUSINESS VISIT:

www.247Runtime.com

IT TROUBLESHOOTING

NETWORK SECURITY

TECH SUPPORT

INSTALLATION / MAINTENANCE

INFRASTRUCTURE DESIGN

IT & SOCAIL MEDIA SUPPORT

Contact: info@247runtime.com